The Odd Collection

SAMANTHA TURNER

ISBN: 978-1-915889-49-2

Contact the author at:
skylarkfiction@gmail.com

PublishNation
www.publishnation.co.uk

Introduction

As a writer, I often find myself with lots of random poems and stories that are quite different from one another in theme and style. This happens because I rarely decide to 'sit down and write' that just doesn't work for me. My words decide themselves when they want to be written and therefore, I have a phone and many notebooks crammed with verses and sentences demanding to be heard. My dilemma begins when I try to group these bossy little scribblings into one coherent book. Finding such a task near impossible with this unruly bunch I decided to title the book accordingly.

Contents

Silvanus

I was once a happy child who ran wild with grubby, bare feet through the bright green woodland. A carefree girl who lay amongst the scented lilac bluebells and heady wild garlic, I didn't care if my long brown hair was tangle-free, or if my fingernails were clean. Now old age had finally caught up with me and I decided it was time to return to that lush woodland, one final time. As I was reaching the end of my life, there was no better place I could have chosen.

I had lived a long life, which even though had included some tragedy, had mostly been blessed with love and friendship. But now I was the only one left. When my husband Jack died that was the beginning of the end for me. We had met as teenagers; I was fifteen and he was nineteen and as soon as I was old enough, we were married. It had been just the two of us ever since and we had been very close. Of course, after Jack's death my friends tried to keep me occupied by rallying around, bringing me casseroles, and inviting me for lunch, but the sadness and emptiness inside me was all-consuming. Then, as days turned into years, one by one my friends also passed away, as our generation began to make way for the next. So why was I still alive and lingering on? I was eighty-seven years old with an aching body and an empty heart. I was just going through the motions of my daily routine. Talking to myself and sleeping most of the day. I felt disappointed each time I woke up.

The red-bricked Victorian townhouse that had once been alive with laughter and conversation, warmth and love slowly turned into a silent and draughty relic with nothing but memories reflecting from photographs, and mirrors that told lies. I would sit in Jack's favourite armchair by the window, running my thumb over the sun-bleached fabric.

I remembered how Jack would absentmindedly trace the pink, flowery patterns of the embroidery on that chair with his old man fingers, and how he would reach out and take my own aged, mottled hands in his. The love between Jack and I remained strong and vibrant, it never faded like the fabric of the chair had.

What must the neighbours with their young children have thought of the old lady with the wild, white hair who watched them with envy from the gloomy window; probably they thought I was a bit eccentric and that's why they never introduced themselves or asked how I was.

I was tired of living, but I dreaded death. What if I suffered when I stopped breathing? Would I be unconscious before then or would I be aware that my heart and lungs were failing? Would I panic? I wished there was some guarantee that I could've just fallen into blissful sleep and never woken up again. I was at the age where death became a constant wish and a constant fear. There was no escaping the insidious dread that haunted me night and day and I just wanted it to be over with. That was when I decided to go back to the forest. It was a glorious spring afternoon, and I closed the blue front door of our house without locking it; there was no point, and let my feeble feet take me back to the only companion I had left. Down the familiar dirt path I walked, through the pretty meadow of white daisies and vivid yellow dandelions, enjoying the feel of the tall grass as it tickled my legs. Along the way, I cherished the warmth of the spring sunshine on my wrinkled face and deeply inhaled the sweet scent of wildflowers. I took photographs of red admiral and cabbage white butterflies with my old

Canon camera, hoping the tiny details of their beautiful symmetry might live on afterwards. How delicate and free they were, content with their fleeting existence. I slowly made my way to a favourite spot by the large old oak tree that stood proudly and protectively by the gentle forest stream with the stepping-stones, the tree that had been my friend for all these years. I laid my palm upon his rough bark and said a silent farewell. I kicked off my sensible shoes and let the fresh spring grass soothe and cool my overheated feet.

The brown, plastic bottle of pills in my pocket rattled impatiently as I struggled into a sitting position on the uneven forest floor. I could feel sadness and self-pity begin to rise from my heart. I was afraid, I didn't want to leave this beautiful earth, but I was so alone. I was so unhappy.

Sitting with my arthritic back against the large trunk of the Oak tree, legs sprawled in front of me, I sat there like a rag doll. I sat there in that idyllic place surrounded by colour and beauty, and I cried; loud, ugly, sobbing that was very undignified.

I imagined shrinking down to a miniature size person and sailing off down the meandering forest stream in a hazelnut shell, far away from all the dread and pain. Wiping the salty tears out of my swollen green eyes, I looked up from the soft mossy ground, and for a moment I thought I must have fallen asleep and was in a wonderful dream. Standing before me on the other side of the water was the most magnificent sight. A regal-looking stag with enormous antlers headed a crowd of curious-looking woodland creatures. His golden chestnut coat shone with a heavenly light and his deep brown eyes fixed upon mine. An abundance of red and grey squirrels, humbug striped badgers, ginger foxes, silky brown mice, and voles. Every

3

kind of woodland bird from tiny treecreepers to colourful jays; a thousand more curious eyes staring right at me.

The stag took a few elegant steps forward into the stream and stopped a little distance from where I was still sitting, frozen with shock but not in fear.

"Rowena, my child. Do not cry so."

The strong, reassuring voice that spoke to me came from the stag. He knew my name. I had no idea how or even what was happening, but somehow this perfect creature seemed familiar to me.

"We are here for you Rowena, the guardians of this ancient place have always been here, waiting for you to return."

With a shaking voice. I asked, "Who are you and how am I able to communicate with you?"

There was a chatter of voices from the gathering of animals behind the stag, who seemed to be their leader, and he turned his handsome face back towards them.

One commanding look from him was all it took for the crowd to return to silent observation.
"My name is Silvanus, and I am the God of the woods. I have been here since the birth of time itself; protecting and keeping this realm secret. The reason that you can understand me, is because I am allowing you to. Although you have visited this place for many years, the time was not right then for us to reveal ourselves. We remained hidden but always watched over and protected you, my child." An overwhelming feeling of recognition and calmness washed over my body like a warm wave. I recalled the many times that I had played under these trees as a child, and when as

4

a teenager I had hidden deep in their shady depths after playing truant from school. With a little embarrassment, I also remembered the secret liaisons of my husband and I when we were still young and in the throes of passion. This vast forest with its secret hiding places and clear streams has always played a part in my life. The woodland and its inhabitants were my life-long friends; always there, dependable and comforting. This was my safe retreat from the real world.

"I know what it is you have come here to do Rowena." Said Silvanus.

"Your body is tired and old, and your soul is weary of solitude. Banlen the wise sent a message to me and I wasted no time in gathering the assembly."

As Silvanus spoke to me, I guiltily fingered the pill bottle.

"Who is Banlen?" I asked.

"Banlen is the Oak tree behind you. He has been your constant friend and guardian since you were a small girl, keeping me informed of your movements whenever you showed up in this part of the forest." He replied.

I was astonished. Turning around to face Banlen, I could suddenly hear a soft whispering and a low humming which I understood was him telling me he loved me.
"Oh, Banlen," I cried. "My faithful friend, thank you for always being there. Thank you! Thank you for your shade and protection. I will always love and remember you."

It was at that moment that Silvanus and all the other animals crossed the stream and a golden Vixen spoke to me.

"This is not goodbye Rowena." Her voice was pure and melodious. "Come; we have something to show you."

The afternoon sun was filtering through the forest canopy, creating freckles of light that danced upon the backs of the woodland creatures as we moved on mass deeper and deeper into the great woodland.

Having left my shoes behind, my bare feet relished the feel of the soft green moss and lichen on the ground beneath them. After a little while, the animals all stopped by a large opalescent pool of water. There were flowers of such bright rainbow colours and enormous green ferns surrounding this mysterious and awe-inspiring place. Deep caves led off from various points around the pool, and lengths of dark green ivy trailed over grey and purple rocks. The birds within our group began to sing, it was the most beautiful sound that I had ever heard. Silvanus approached my stunned person and told me to enter the water. I felt no fear in doing this and did not hesitate. As my feet broke the surface of the shining liquid, it surprised me that the water was warm and silky. It was like stepping into a bath of cool but molten silver. I stood still and turned my head to look at Silvanus as he spoke to me.

"You are standing in the Pool of Paradise, and you have now entered the Realm of Peace. Please, my child, gaze at your reflection and tell me what you see."

I looked down into the silvery pool and gasped. Staring up at me was my younger self. My white hair was once again long and brown. My skin was peachy pink and plump and wrinkle-free. My eyes were as bright as emeralds and shone back at me with delight. "I am young! I am a girl again, Silvanus, but how can this be?"

6

Unable to tear myself away from the vision in the water, I suddenly heard a deep and joyful laugh come from the benevolent stag. Then all the other animals joined in, and I too became infected by the merriment in the air, laughing as I had never laughed in years. I felt so light and so free.

"Forgive me, Rowena. I had better explain everything." Said Silvanus with obvious mirth in his voice.

"You have reached a grand old age, reserved only for the privileged of your kind. But now you find yourself alone and live each day in fear. You came here to end your life, unable to bear the loneliness and pain any longer. You hoped that those pills you had in your pocket would send you off peacefully into oblivion and death; You were right.

Banlen watched as you swallowed the entire bottle of pills using water from the stream. Banlen supported your frail, dying body as it slumped against his trunk. Once it was over, he sent for me to bring you home."

I felt in my pocket for the bottle of morphine pills; it was empty. I tried to think back to when I arrived in the woods. I remembered crying one minute and then seeing Silvanus the next. I looked at my hands, not as a reflection but as my real hands. They were the hands of a girl. I lifted a leg out of the water and that also was a young, healthy leg with muscle tone and strength. I ran my fingers through my hair and felt the once familiar thickness and soft curls. I couldn't help myself, I shrieked with delight! I jumped and splashed as my pain-free body was overcome with happiness. I felt as light as a feather and as free as a bird! The animals all rushed to join me in the water and the birds fluttered and danced around me in joy.

"Does this mean what I think it means Silvanus?" I asked. My voice was clear and youthful.

"Yes Rowena, your mortal body died when the pills entered your bloodstream. Banlen will keep your physical remains buried beneath his roots, forever protected and your grave will never be discovered by any living person. All that will be found are your shoes and the camera. Your disappearance will be a mystery."

"I expect no one will even notice I have gone," I replied.

"There is someone who has been waiting for you, Rowena. They have been among us in the Realm of Peace for some time, although time does not exist here as it does in the human world. You will never age or feel pain here. There is no death or fear in the Realm of Peace, and it is always spring. You are free to enjoy this Eden and you will never again be alone. Most importantly, Rowena, you will always, always have love."

Silvanus' words filled me with hope but also confusion. I was dead, at least my decrepit body was, and I was happy and relieved about that. But who else was here in this place of wonder and enchantment? In life I had never known my parents, they had been killed in the war when I was a baby and I had been brought up in a foster home in the countryside. Jack had died from a heart attack in our back garden when he was eighty. So, who did I know that could have died in these woods?

Stepping out of the water, I sat down next to a rotund-looking badger, his black and white wiry coat a contrast to the bright green grass, and he handed me a ruby red strawberry the size of an apple. If only I could describe the sweetness and juiciness of that first bite but there are no words that could do the fruity deliciousness any real justice. This must be heaven I thought, or at least it was my heaven. I didn't know where everyone else went after they died. To think how terrified I had been of dying; gosh, if only I had known! I felt like all the weight of life and death had just been cut from me and I had floated away from it like a balloon set free. All that fear and worrying over dying now seemed like such a pointless waste of earthly energy.

Most of the other animals were sleeping peacefully now and I laid my head down on the soft fur of a rabbit called Renshay, who had snuggled up in my nest of hair.

A shadow passed before my closed eyes and upon opening them I saw Silvanus' perfect shape standing over me.

"Rowena my child, I must leave you now. I will be back from time to time, but this realm is vast, as you will discover for yourself; and I have many more children who need my guidance. However, I will be leaving you in the companionship of all your brothers and

sisters whom you have already become acquainted with. I also have a gift for you before I depart."

With this said, the mighty stag moved aside. A boy about my age stood with a large smile on his youthful face. He had blonde hair the colour of straw and eyes as blue as the ocean. He was wearing clothes made of some soft, mossy material which I realised was the same shade of green as the shift dress that I wore. He may only have been a boy now, but I recognized him at once.

"Alright, Wenny?" Said Jack. Wenny was what he used to call me. "I've been waiting for you, isn't this wonderful?"

We ran into each other's arms, and he smelled of sweet peas and earthy soil.

"Oh, Jack my love, look at us! We are young, forever young Jack! And we are together in this paradise." I was so happy and overcome with love at the sight of Jack but how did he get there?

"Jack passed away over by the Apple-blossom trees at the bottom of your garden." Answered Silvanus in his velvety voice.

"When Jack's lifeforce left his body, it travelled down into the soil and was taken in by the tree roots. The roots passed Jack's energy along the underground system until it reached Banlen in the forest. Banlen being the wise tree he is, knew who Jack was and I allowed him to become part of the Realm of Peace."

Having watched us in the forest over the long years of our lives together, walking and talking, laughing, and paddling, sleeping and loving, Silvanus and the other creatures of the forest knew that Jack and I were two souls destined to be together, always.

Jack took my glowing face in his young hands and kissed me gently, his pillow-soft lips tasted like sweet honey. A ray of golden light emanated from our spiritual bodies as the love between us shone. Turning to face the water, we watched together as the mighty stag Silvanus disappeared into a dark cave on the far side of the pond. We didn't feel sad, it was impossible to feel anything but joy in the Realm of Peace.

"Come on Wenny," said Jack. "There's so much that I want to show you." So, hand in hand we ran, through the endless carpet of bluebells, never to be parted again.

11

Bygone times

"Nan will tell me the story about how you met grandad," I asked the kind-looking old lady as she passed me my milky cup of tea; served with a small spoon like she used to when I was little so I could drink it like soup.

"Oh, that was such a long time ago Emma and your granddad's been gone nearly six years now. Though I'll never forget the first time I saw Tom. He was quite a catch you know! Go on then, make yourself comfortable by the fire and I'll tell you what I remember."

I was fifteen years old when my mam sent me to work over at the John pit. I could've gone to the cotton mill, but the pit was within walking distance to our house on Woodcock row in Crooke village. Most of the local lads worked in the pit and so did my dad before he died young of lung disease, leaving my mam to support me and herself on her own. I didn't mind going out to work, mam did her best for us and always had a hot meal of potato pie or bread and cheese waiting after a hard day. Sometimes if it were a special occasion, she'd make fruit cake and custard, which was a real treat!

Grafting at the pit was difficult and grubby but, despite not being allowed to talk to each other while we were working, me and my friend Annie still had a bit of a giggle at times when we thought no one was looking. We even learned how to lip-read so we could silently communicate.

Our job as pit brow lasses was to wait for the coal to come in from the shaft below, then we had to pick out the dirt and stones so they wouldn't explode when the coal went into the fire. All the bits that we pulled out just got thrown onto the floor so, after a while, we'd have to stop and shovel it all up or it'd be piled high over our boots! It was bloody cold in winter, we had gloves, but they had no fingers in them because we had to work fast with our hands. We wore head scarves and shawls and heavy woollen skirts which were warm but felt like they were dragging you down when they got wet. Mam said they were hard to wash and dry those wool skirts. Remember, in those days there were no fancy washing machines. It was all done by hand on wash day once a week.

One cold October morning in 1948, I was eighteen by then and there was a new lad just started at our John pit. Tommy Fisher was his name. He'd moved from Haigh with his old grandad and lived in Standish Lower Ground now. Soon as me and Annie set eyes on him, we were as giddy as two schoolgirls. Tommy was dark and handsome with eyelashes any girl would have died for. Even the coal dirt on his face didn't take away his good looks. It was impossible dressed as we were to look pretty, but I did my best to make sure I always had a smile when he looked my way.

That autumn was a real wet one and as I was leaving the site one gloomy night, thinking about my tea and a warm brew, I suddenly slipped in the mud and landed heavily on my backside in a heap. Dirty, wet, and feeling like a right fool I struggled to pick myself up from the slippery ground. I looked up to see a strong, calloused hand grabbing mine and my eyes met those long lashes of Tommy Fisher. Like my knight in a flat cap, he graciously helped me to my wobbly feet and we both had a chuckle; once I'd got over the shame. Once he'd made sure that I wasn't hurt, Tommy insisted on walking me home even though it was out of his way. The conversation came easily between us as Tommy was very down-to-earth and friendly. I found out he was twenty years old, and he was a 'hooker on' which meant he worked at the bottom of the mine shaft hooking on the cages filled with coal and sending them up to the surface. Tommy was not only handsome but also kind and funny. I was smitten. Luckily for me, he seemed to feel the same way and our walking home and little chats became a regular occurrence. Annie was jealous as hell at first but after a while, she started courting a lad from Shevington, so she soon lost interest in us. We stayed friends though and would both dream about getting married and living next door to each other, our kids playing together like we had done when we were growing up.

Life went on this way, and we were happy. It didn't seem to matter that we were poor. We had a job, a home, food on the table and fierce friendships. People stuck together back then and wouldn't hesitate to help a neighbour in need. Our little community up North revolved around the coal pit, the school, and the Methodist meetings at the village chapel.

One Saturday when I'd finished my shift I walked home on my own, Tommy had told me the day before that he had to stay on a bit later that night. I was tired but content and it was Sunday tomorrow which meant a chapel meeting but a day off from the pit. As I made my way through the rusty iron gate up to our weather-worn front door, I heard voices in the front room. When I walked in, I was surprised to see my mam sitting by the fire with Tommy. They'd met briefly before, but I wouldn't have said they were pals. They both looked startled to see me standing there and Tommy immediately rose from the sofa; I noticed he had been sitting in dad's old spot.

"Here's our Eileen now," said mam. "Tommy's come round to ask me something and he seems like an honest, hardworking lad so I've said yes. I think your dad would've agreed, God rest his soul."

Tommy looked at me and I looked back in bewilderment.

"Eileen," he said. "I know I've not much, but I think the world of you, and I've put a bit by so we can get wed if you want to like?"

A laugh of shock and surprise burst from my mouth, "Yes," I said.

I ran into his arms and then quickly pulled away again as my mam gave us a disapproving look.

"There'll be time for all that once you're married. We'll speak to the vicar after service tomorrow and Tommy, I'll need to meet your grandad."

A month later Tommy and I became husband and wife at a simple ceremony in the village chapel. I felt beautiful in mam's wedding dress, white cotton with a simple pale blue ribbon around the waist and a chain of daisies in my mousey brown hair that Annie had styled into soft curls for me. It poured down with rain but still, all the families came out to see us, and mam put on a small spread of sandwiches and cake with a little fruit cordial and tea for everyone.

I moved into the house that Tommy lived in with his grandad. The house wasn't much bigger than mams, but grandad couldn't be left alone. Tommy and me had our own bedroom at least and there was a separate parlour with a pantry. It was decided that I would leave my job at the pit to take care of the house, and grandad. Mam was sad to see me leave but I visited her almost every day. She got a few hours of work a week cleaning at the village school so was able to support herself financially. I was happy with my lot and Annie would come for a brew and tell me any gossip from the village. Cooking and cleaning also kept me busy.

One evening I was laying the table with crusty homemade bread and thick, creamy butter, waiting for Tommy to come home from work. He always said the delicious smell of stew cooking on the stove wafted down the street as he made his way to the house. I looked at the clock and noticed Tommy was a bit late. It wasn't like him to be late, but I wasn't too worried at that point. I was just giving the stew a final stir when suddenly in the distance I heard the ominous sound of a horn, it came from the pit. I ran outside to find that most of the neighbours were already out. Something was wrong. There had been an accident at John pit. My stomach sank and my legs had a mind of their own. I ran and ran, heart, pounding in my chest until I reached the pit. The rain was lashing down and I was soaked to the skin but all I felt was panic and numbness. It was chaos. Men were dragging limp and blackened bodies from underground, unrecognisable, covered in coal dirt and mud. Women were screaming and being held back by some of the older lads.

"Where is my Tommy?" I cried, "Annie, Tommy!"

I sank to my knees in despair. He was dead. I knew it in my heart. My Tommy had been crushed by a collapse in the mine. My darling, beautiful husband. The rain had weakened the tunnel structure and the men couldn't escape in time. I must have fallen into a daze when I was roughly shaken back to the moment by Annie.
"Eileen, what are you doing? Tommy needs you. Snap out of it."

16

Hearing Tommy's name and Annie's voice sparked a flame inside me, and we ran together over to where a group of exhausted-looking men were sitting by the sheds. There was my Tommy. Bruised, bloody, but alive! I threw my arms around him and sobbed.

"Easy lass, I'm alright, I'm alright," he said in a hoarse whisper.

Six lads lost their lives that day. One was from our village. He was only sixteen and named Billy Halsall, mam and me used to see him and the others at the chapel. There was a memorial service and later a plaque was erected with the names of those poor souls who had died. The loss hit the village hard, but the mine was soon back up and running. Coal mining was the livelihood of nearly everyone and people just couldn't afford to leave, despite the risk. It was one of many mining tragedies that happened in various coal mines up North and even though the mine owners made changes, accidents still happened, and people still died.

Your grandad, Tommy, was incredibly lucky. He managed to get out as he was working near the entrance, but he was saddened by the loss of his pals. Right up until his own death as an old man he'd still visit that memorial plaque and run his fingers over the names. He used to say that you never really forget a tragedy like that, no matter how many years may pass.

Well, as you know your grandad and me remained in Wigan here in Standish Lower Ground all our lives and had your dad and your auntie Betty. As it turned out Annie got married and had two sons. They moved into the house next door, and we'd chat over the fence while the kids played in the garden. It was a simple life, but we were happy with what we had and never imagined wanting more.

Tommy and me were married for fifty-two years and I know that he's up there waiting for me with his long lashes and a loving hand to pull me up to heaven.

Spring for the very first time

The Winter darkness I used to
dread
For the terrors would haunt me
then
I was a prisoner trapped inside my own
head
No escape and nowhere to
run

My petals seemed always to be
wilted
All colours around me
subdued
The light outside could not reach
me
From the living, I was too far
removed

I could find no joy in
beauty
Birdsong became only
noise
Raindrops would no longer soothe
me
In fear, my hollow stem
recoiled

But I am tough because I am
fragile
My strength was just buried
deep
I only needed to rest
awhile
In safe, restorative
sleep

Gentle rain upon dry
lips
Awoke me from dark
despair
From Earth and sky, I took a
sip
And inhaled the sweetened
air

The flowers all bloomed
And danced with
mirth
As the clouds of sorrow
parted
Emerging like a second
birth
I arose all joyful
hearted

The sky had never been so
blue
The sun never shone so
bright
Breaking through my unhappy
cocoon
It was like spring for the very first time

The artist

There is no artist quite as
fine
As one who paints with brush
divine
With every stroke, they mould and shape
With every flick they
animate

Imagination knows no
bounds
From empty easel life
astounds
Our mortal talents, dull and
mild
Cannot compare to wonders
wild
Their rivers round and smooth the
stones
Which lie on bed and
bank
Their golden skies ignite the
clouds
And warm the velvet
flank
Of stag who proud and regal
stands
So true in form and
colour
A stroke of brown, a white
highlight
An image like no
other

Such talent that can conjure
life
With mere pencil, brush and
paint
Must surely be from Heaven
sent
To share this gift so
great!

Childhood memories

I used to love the summer holidays when I was little.
The seemingly endless warm days and freedom to play.
To get muddy, dig up clay
and shape it into animals brought to life by my own
imagination.
Lying in the village park, bright green grass stains on
white socks,
making daisy chains that would never last and blowing the
time away on dandelion clocks.
My childhood memories of summer
are always lit with the yellow
memory of twirling
buttercups under our chin to see if we liked butter.

What is a dream?

What is a dream?
Just thoughts from the
day
Jumbled up and
replayed
As a film on the waves in our
brain?

A cinematic slide of the unconscious
mind
Creating nonsense of memories remade?

Do our souls awaken while our mortal
bodies rest?
Do our spirits dance and
play
With the ones we thought were dead?

But dreams are thin and merely wisps
Of scenes we cannot
hold
For when we wake and eyes
forget
The curtain falls once
more

That clock

Tick tock, tick tock
There it goes stealing my time
Gone, gone
With every second, with every chime
It used to be silent that clock
Before I noticed it
Even though I was travelling fast, so fast
That clock remained unheard
Not now.
Now I hear it
Loud like thunder, like waves
Ticking, always ticking
Counting down to my demise
When did I first hear it, that clock?
Was it when the music died?
Maybe
That was when the thoughts began
That was when I realised

Lucky clovers

I found two lucky four-leaf clovers today, they were just sitting there in plain sight. So many childhood minutes I had searched unsuccessfully through the millions to find just one. Now I had found two without even trying, growing in our back garden among the wispy dandelion clocks. See what treasure appears when we don't mow the grass.

I was quite excited at my rare find and it was the first thing I told you when you walked through the door. "Right" was all you said in response.

Perhaps your Nan didn't win £800 at bingo when you were little after she found a giant four-leaf clover, that forever after she kept in a clear plastic keyring attached to her purse. Maybe your Mum and Dad never sat in the long green grass of Springs gone by helping you to search and search for the elusive lucky charm.

It's wonderful how this tiny green plant can transport me back to a time and place where I am once again a giggling child, who still sees the world as a fairy-tale full of magic and possibilities.

I left the four-leaf clovers in the ground to live on. However, should I hear the death roar of the lawnmower man I shall run outside to rescue them and preserve their rare form in a miniature plastic museum for all eternity.

The circus

In 1930 when I was aged ten
We were lodgers in a cottage
Just me and my gran
My mother had left to live out of town
I didn't want to go, and dad wasn't around

Times were tough, but so was Gran
We always had enough, and I would lend a hand
With cooking and cleaning and laundry day
Then when it was finished, I could go out to play

The fields at the back were vast and green
I would run fast through the meadows
Feeling happy and free

One summer morning there was excitement and clatter
I looked out the window, stood on a chair to see better

Right there in the field, not believing my eyes
Was an enormous tent with strange people outside

Such rainbow colours and bright fancy clothes
Feathers, sequins, and diamonds on show

There were crazy-looking men with white faces, red lips
Beautiful dancers doing cartwheels and flips

Some wearing tights with large black moustaches
One wheeled bikes and many pretend crashes

I leapt from the chair and ran to the field
Eager to get there, I wanted to see

More of this wonder, what was all this raucous?
Then a loud voice behind me said
"Welcome to the circus!"

Aggie Brown

She lives in a hut in a woodland glade
Built from tarpaulin and roughly made
Her clothes are worn with patches sewn
To cover the holes and keep out the cold

Known in town as Aggie Brown
An enigma to all, her story unknown

One boot is green and the other bright blue
Picking mushrooms in the forest
Making potions and stew

A hat made of tin foil she wears on her head
To protect against mind control
"From the Aliens," she said

But our old Aggie, she does no harm
She's just a little eccentric from living alone
So, if I see Aggie, I'll give her a smile
Ask how she is and talk for a while
She could shy away and maybe ignore me
But there's just a small chance
I might learn her story

Lost at sea

We are drawn to the sea
Like the tides to the moon
Tethered by some silvery thread

Back and forth go we
Compelled by the Siren's tune
"Return, return" she sings
As back to the sea we are led

Our salty tears add to the swell
Gulls cry above translucent waves
"Turn back," they say
"All is not well you are going to your grave"

An intermittent lighthouse-beam
Reminds us of land and home
Illuminating our trance-like dream
And the hypnotic ebb and flow

Of tides that wish to take us yet
On mighty crescents of thunder
Washed down to deep and inky depths
To claim us like Pirates' plunder

Sinking ever further there
A violent beauty glows
To trick us to her deadly lair
Amidst the sailors' bones

Unearthly pleasure, this song so sweet
Odysseus resist the call
For to listen is to surely meet
The death and loss of all!

Sunken wrecks a prison make
For victims of the Siren
From which there can be no escape
No one shall hear them crying

So, remember on that sunny day
When calm and soothing tides
Seem harmless or that murky cave
Entices you inside

Keep your wits and listen now
This warning I give to thee
Beware the enchanting Siren's call
Or be forever lost at Sea!

Flip-flops

You can't walk proudly in Flip-flops
No matter how hard you might try
The best you will manage is a curious waddle
Like a duck who's unable to fly

You can't walk quietly in Flip-flops
And don't even think about running
With each shameful slap, slap
They're a rubber death trap
And everyone nearby hears you coming

You can't possibly be comfy in
Flip-flops
A thong for your toes is just wrong
You shuffle and slide causing blisters inside
In the bin is where Flip-flops belong!

Alone in a coffee shop

Sat alone in a coffee shop
Staring at the wall
It's too hot in here
And I've been seduced by the vegan sausage roll

I'm paranoid, people watching me eat
Crumbs and filling squidging as I take a bite
Loud conversations, sighs, and indignation
A snippet of someone else's life

How difficult; do they want a regular or a large?
"Why can they not do a small?
Moans Carol
"Ask that girl, she looks in charge."

Now the card machine is broken,
This has ruined her day
Carol doesn't carry cash
Contactless is how she wanted to pay

I smile to myself as Carol makes a fuss,
Her daughter is clearly mortified
I ponder, shall I walk home or catch the bus?
While brushing the pastry crumbs away from my thighs

I finish my latte, leaving a drop
I never see the bottom of a cup
I've got a two-mile walk home, and it's started to rain
Fasten my coat and hood up

Covid shopping

Sat in a café among the brave and defiant
Conspiracy theories and dark looks are flying
She's not in a mask, avoid her like a zombie
Quick, get the hand gel and squirt it upon me!

Everyone shuffling along in a line
Keeping their distance in frustrating time
One-way systems, wait your turn
Eager shoppers, patience must learn

Hands in your pockets look with your eyes
For whatever you touch you now must buy

Going the wrong way down the supermarket aisle
Head hung in shame like I'm committing a crime

I've forgotten the salad, but I'm near the bread
No turning back, follow the arrows they said

Grab the salad, spin around the trolley
Get back in procession maybe nobody saw me

No time for browsing, I must be fast
There's someone behind me swearing in their mask
They want to look in the whoopsie crate
But keeping safe distance means they just have to wait

Screens at the checkout, cash is the devil
You better pay by card or face the wrath of Beryl!
Eyes glaring over mask and screen
"Contactless only"
Shouts the muffled scream

What an ordeal, so stressful and judgy
Never again, I'd rather go hungry!

Used

To only be needed but never wanted
To be treated as a final resort
You think my feelings are reusable
I am just a forgotten after-thought

When you had no one, I was there
I never left you behind
For I didn't want you to be lonely
I gave you my friendship and time

Is there a reason that you have forgotten?
Or do you believe your own lies?
Do our memories mean so little?
Has tunnel vision made you blind?

Maybe I am just a fool
Perhaps I care too much
I believed you would just love me
After all, we share the same blood

Well now I've given up
You will never really change
I have exhausted all my hope
And things shall never be the same

Time mimicking time

The low hum of a kettle boiling,
Middle-aged fingers dip into the tea-bag pot
The tinny clinking of the spoon on cups.
Eyes watching the clock

Not quite yet, the tea will be too cold,
The sound of a key turning in the lock

The light comes on as the fridge door opens, pour in the
Milk now
He is home and the tea is just right

He smells of machines and sweat,
His calloused hands with rough bitten nails wrap
Gratefully around the steaming cup

A tired smile and closed eyes as she asked
"How was your day love?"
With a hint of guilt in her voice

I view these images now as they were, like cinematic
Slides of a child's mind

Now it is not my mother who stands by the kettle each
Night, it is me
The fingers that wrap around the cup are still calloused
And bitten but they are not my father's, they belong to my
Husband.

A memory repeated, relieved
Time mimicking time

Here we go again

Here we go again feeling trapped and restricted
Counting down the days until the lock-down rules are
lifted

Not all can blow a bubble or online shop in which to
spend
Instead, the darkness has consumed them
As Summer reached the end

Do not let the winter gloom be a cause for fear and dread
We must have hope each morning
No matter what, get out of bed

Let each new day be a blessing
We are here, we are alive
The birds are still out there singing
Open the door, look up to the sky

Put on your warmest jacket
Take a coffee out to the garden
Appreciate the simple pleasures
Breath in deep and ease the burden

And when the night draws in
Put on the cosy little lamps
Find new friends inside a story
Or play your favourite song and dance!

A groovy old lady

I'll be a groovy old lady
With long wavy hair down my back
I might leave it grey or not care what they say and wear it
bright pink in a plait

I'll be a groovy old lady
In blue jeans and Doc Martin boots
I'll listen to 90's rave,
Drink beer and misbehave
And refuse to let go of my youth

I'll be a groovy old lady
And lie on the beach all day long
I'll sip dry Martini in my tight thong bikini
And won't give A damn what they think

I'll be a groovy old lady
The reaper will save me for last
Then he'll say
"Come on trouble, I've bought you a double. It looks like
Your life was a blast!"

The bouncy ball song

Most couples in love have a song,
We don't.
We danced to Enrique Iglesias at our wedding, a song that
you chose.
'I will be your hero'
I used to hear it played on the radio when I was at work,
and I would wonder if you were listening to the same
station.
Were you also feeling the nostalgia and thinking of me at
that very same moment?
No. You don't remember Enrique. You thought we had
danced to
'The bouncy ball song'
Then you laughed and I laughed too, but inside I was a
little hurt.
You are still my hero though.
'The bouncy ball song'
We never knew who sang it. It was just an advert on the
TV with lots of multi-colored bouncy balls jumping down
some steep American street.
I said,
"I like this song"
and you said,
"So do I."

My old road

My old road, my street, my home
Low garden fences and steps of stone
The red brick houses that all look alike
Mums chatting on the front was a regular sight

My grandma's house right at the top
The woodpigeon calling and the gentle ticking clock

Playing outside, eating chips in a bag
Didn't want to go in, so much fun to be had

Just a bunch of kids all from the same road
Some round the corner and others lived next door

Riding our bikes and making dens
I'll never forget my childhood friends
I didn't know then how we would all grow
That mum and dad would change and get old

I'm married now, I have moved away
But that old road has barely changed
Those kids, now adults some live nearby
Their parents still live there, as do mine

That road, those kids will always be
My home, my heart, my memories

Warm cup

Warm cup, cold hands
Wrapped around fingers burn numbly
Such comfort hides the pain
That will come later, and regret will follow
As it always does

Lazy Sunday

No alarm, no morning dread
Wake up late, have coffee in bed
Stretch and yawn then snuggle back down
No judgement here, it's Sunday I'm
allowed

The rain is pouring, it's good for the flowers
No need to get dressed, I'll spend some lazy hours
Reading quietly with a pot of tea
And a packet of biscuits, all for me

The gentle ticking clock, the turn of a page
With the background music of the pattering rain

A perfect day for idleness, for peace, rest, and quietness
Breath in deep and close your eyes
Let this lazy Sunday dream on by

Fallen apples

Fallen apples wasting among decaying leaves
Red, green, orange, and brown
Sweet, putrid flesh feeding the ground

Did I fall or was I picked?
Either way, I'm a little bruised
I wish I had been higher up, desired but never used

Like the big, confident red apples
That everyone wants but cannot reach
Provocatively bathed in golden dapples from light above

But then,
Those apples don't live on in jam, cake, and pies
I wouldn't have had any fun
If I'd been left up there to die

Once a ripe and juicy ornament
Now shrivelled up and rotten
No longer full and succulent
Just lonely and forgotten

All hallows eve

I have been waiting all year
For this night
Enduring the long summer
Impatiently
But now it is finally here
I am afraid

Before you crossed
Over
You asked me to
Wait
On all hallows eve
At the chime of midnight

The clock hands are
Ticking
Will I feel your hands in
Mine?
What if you do not
Appear
When I have waited all this
Time?

With the thinning, of the
Veil
You will step out from the
Ether
My heartbeat to guide your
Way
Then we shall be
Together

We will only have the
Darkness
Before you must
Return
Then another endless
Year
Until I see my love again

Always remember

Today I am closing my eyes
Remembering the fear of the brave
As they willingly signed up to die
No matter the horrors they faced

With dignity and silence
Mothers held back the tears
Though dying inside
They must not see her fears

The lads from the village
The Pals and the brothers
Went to fight for their country
For freedom and each other

How many came home?
So many bereft
Changed and haunted men
Replaced the boys who left

Today I am listening out for the cries
For the echo of grenades and gunshots
I try
To imagine the smell of the trenches and smoke
As one after one up and over they go

The terror and the glory
Like twisted barbed wire
Of battlefields fought
By those aching and tired

So, today I am closing my eyes
Remembering with honour them all
The soldiers, the horses, the pigeons, and dogs
Each one a hero who helped fight for us

I shall always remember with love and gratitude
I am here, I am free, and it is all thanks to you

9/11

I can only imagine the absolute fear
Of the desperate souls as the plane drew near
The frantic calls and farewell texts
No time left for things unsaid

Observers in horror from down below
Are shocked and helpless as the terror unfolds
The second tower, the falling man,
Screams, disbelief; they cannot save them

Anger and flames, panic and chaos
The realisation of loved ones lost
In the aftermath, the weeping sky
An entire world left wondering why?

Every year, 11th of September
Take a quiet moment to honour and remember
The brave, the strong, the frightened, the lost
So, we never forget the individual
Cost
Of every family, friend and
Lover
Who's patched up heart will never recover

Winter

I put on my hat and coat
Still yawning
And step out into the wind and cold of the
Indigo morning
Where the first imprints in the sleeping snow
Are my own

I feel the breath of winter
As her frigid kisses on my frozen cheeks
Linger
Then her caress as an icy
Finger
Traces the length of my shivering spine

I wrap my comforting scarf
A little tighter around my face
And willingly I go
Into Lady Winters' cold embrace
I see beauty in the snowflakes
As they drift and dance and sway
Each one an individual
You will find no two the same

Bereft trees are outlined in white
Their leaves lie rigid on the ground
Almost ethereal like
With a frosty skeleton endowed

A fallen log I find
Amid the still abeyance
With warm cup in cold hands
I covet my steaming coffee

This day of peace is almost done
And dark is closing in
Time to rouse and head for home
To thaw my frozen limbs

A winter scene

The winter sky is dense with white heavy clouds
There will be snow tonight
And we shall wake
To a quilt of shimmering silence blanketing the land

One intricate, unique pattern
Started it all
By falling softly
Followed by another
And from that other followed more

Dotted among waxy spikes
Are colours of red and green
Though encased in her overcoat of white
The Holly is mostly unseen

Twig-like footprints
Of lightly hopping birds
Indent the unspoilt canvas
Creating pretty patterns and swirls

My warm breath lingers
In icy air for a moment
I blow on my frozen fingers
Trying in vain to warm them

This scene of perfect winter
I want it to remain
Just a little longer
Before it is discovered
And it is not just mine
Anymore

Making merry

Fatty treats and Christmas spirits
My favourite dress, I can't fit in it
Festive excuses and making merry
All contributed to my enormous belly

My hips have grown extensively
My thighs have spread a mile
This body grows more voluptuous
With every Greggs mince pie

I can't resist the Baileys
The crackers or the cheese
I have to live in leggings
Now I can't zip up my jeans

Photos are a nightmare
I'll hide behind the tree
And cover all the mirrors
To hide myself from me

If only I had self-control
To resist all this temptation
To favour what's in the fruit bowl
instead of the celebrations

Oh well, I'm fat, it's too late now
I'll diet after Christmas
So, roll me to the mistletoe
And I'll kiss my favourite biscuit!

Christmas is over

Christmas is over, the chaos is done
The house is a mess and I now weigh a tonne
Both presents and food were all received well
But now comes normality and the credit card bill

I feel a bit deflated, and the weather is mild
I long for the snow like a disappointed child

New Year's Eve is never what it seems
And it's just another night in the grand old- scheme of
Things

We countdown to midnight
Then watch glitter bombs light the sky
Lovers kiss the new year in
And we all sing Auld lang syne

Falling into bed just like we did last year
Somehow feels different
As we shed a little tear

For alcohol and memories can make a melancholy brew
If we dwell on should have,
Could have been
Instead of dreams anew

So, raise a glass up to the stars
Keep hope inside your heart
Fear not that things are ending
As it's really, just the start

Echo

Wild and free in this green glade
I dance beneath the leafy shade
Between shadow shapes and golden rays
On cool and velvet moss I lay
To close my eyes at peace, serene
Bright fragrant flowers ignite my dream
A meadow lit by amber glow
Honeysuckle, Orchid, and Marigold

The trees delight, the butterflies too
As undisturbed this sparkling dew
Of morning spring bursts into being
Buzzing, fluttering, humming, and singing

Cool and clear oh gentle brook
My fallen grace your current took
When sweetened breeze upon my brow
Did breathe away my daisy crown

So rich the emerald sea of ferns
On hillside swell with ardent yearning
To conquer field and forest glade
Before the autumn brings decay

As morning fades and noon recedes
I sense upon the twilight breeze
A foreboding cloud, the air of change
The distant roar of impatient rage

The storm is moving, racing wild
I open my arms, I feel alive
Eat the thunder and drink the rain
I am Nature and cannot be tamed

Fierce yet swift the angry weather
Swayed yellow gorse and lilac heather
An earthy scent of petrichor rises from the ancient moor

Sapphire darkness, petals close
Glittering silver from Heaven arose
All is quiet, silent, and still
Until the sound of the Vixen; shrill
A ghostly white before my eyes
The majestic Barn owl glides on by

I feel it all, the Earth vibrating
Tree, soil, energy shaking
Through my bones and through my mind
For I am Echo Nature's child!

Imagine a rainforest

Imagine if you can, a lush and vibrant forest
Rich in green of every shade, yet untouched by man

A tropical rainbow paradise, a kaleidoscope delight
Made magic by the heavy rains that bring this realm to life

Imagine if you're able, a cascade of crashing water
Thundering overleaf and edge of Mother nature's table

Life abundant tree and floor
Flowers bright and fauna glow
Chainsaws, chopping, habitats gone
Ignorance and greed, the disease of man

Imagine if you can, an Eden turned to dust
A silent, colourless wasteland no oxygen; no, us

A prophecy

I cut my hand Today
On a small glass garden lantern, I only felt the sting of
Pain
Once I saw that it was broken
And the blood ran red
Into the rivulets of my palm
A river of fate it could be said
As into my lifeline, it ran
For there, the blood stopped dead
Congealed into a sticky dam
A prophecy of what lies ahead
Or just a small wound on my hand?

The bluebells

The Bluebells have returned for me
They know how I await
Their violet-scented sanctuary
To transform this forest glade

Winter after winter since ancient times of old
They silently have slumbered
Beneath the solid cold

Quietly they whisper now
A lullaby in my head
And dozily I drift on down
Into my Bluebell bed

Garlic white and Anemone
Protect my tranquil rest
The chiffchaff and the Robin
Singling proudly overhead

Oh, leave me in my happy place
Surrounded by old friends
Who wrap me in their calm embrace
where I am home again

Darling Daisy

Beneath the feathery icy blades
Of grass that should be green
Is a confused little Daisy
Not a sight in Winter seen

Her petals are lithe and graceful
Adorned with a frosty veil
A spring bride wed in winter
She didn't want to wait

Good luck my darling Daisy
I respect your hardy grace
To fight through solid ground
Into winter's cold embrace

You and I

Under the same moon
You and I shone
We gazed upon the same stars with wonder
But on time's gentle breeze
You drifted one way and I in the other

I waited for you under the Willow tree
Until the clocks began to fly
Where the dandelions found you
And whispered my name into the sky

You had been searching for me; all this time
Then you found me by the Willow tree
And put your hand in mine

Next door's washing

Next door's washing is
Waving at me from the grey whirligig
Trying to catch my gaze
As I look around, I see them
Like pastel-coloured criminals punished for how they
Misbehaved
What kind of crime could leggings commit?
Did they stretch too far up
Revealing that 'camel toe' bit?
Did the cardigan lose a button?
Did the white jeans get a stain?
They must have done something terrible to face all this
Disdain
Did the poor clothing know
That the worst was yet to come?
Torture by hot iron
If only they could run
Just then a gust of mighty wind blew suddenly from the
West
The whirligig spun violently
And the clothes became un-fast
Upon the air, the fugitives flew
As their jailer watched on in vain
A pair of pink panties shouted
"knickers to you"
And proceeded with their daring escape!

More by this author

My Heart On Your Sleeve

The Rhymes In My Mind

Ingram Content Group UK Ltd.
Milton Keynes UK
UKHW052125100323
418325UK00003B/6